The Story of Wicken Coronation Band 1911 – 2011

by
Arthur Scrivener
Anthony Day
C J Palmer

First published 2011

Jill Rogers Associates Limited
6 The Maltings, Millfield
Cottenham
Cambridge CB24 8RE
www.jillrogersassociates.co.uk

ISBN 978-0-9560156-5-5

British Library Cataloguing in Publication Data. A catalogue record for this book is available for the British Library.

Typeset in Garamond
Printed by Burlington Press, Cambridge

Introduction

Born of an age of self-provision and self-entertainment, Wicken Coronation Band has survived through a period of lost institutions and services and the gradual decline in its local population. Heading for its centenary as I write, it has been boosted in recent years by its appeal to the young, providing them with a practical way into music not on offer in many of our villages today.

It has, of course, ridden many a crisis though, between and after two world wars but each time found the will to carry on and excel, any show of dissent or temperament eased away in the cause.

During the latter part of its history we have lost our cherished school, our village shops, our resident vicar, our Women's Institute while the religious institutions have struggled to survive and there is a lot more to keep people at home and away from our excellent Village Hall when the Band performs there. Oddly at this time they are more gratefully received in neighbouring villages that once had their own bands.

This Village Hall, once a second church built for accessibility in 1887, is where the Band practises every week helped by the acoustics. Long ago they practised in the clubroom of The Maid's Head and my clearest memory is of the then bandmaster carrying his instrument across Cross Green in front of my home, a man who was to declare his commitment to the Band in no uncertain way.

Fourteen years my near neighbour, his name was Arthur Scrivener, and I had to wait some forty years to discover his allegiance. He was living in retirement in Soham having just lost his wife. We came together on the topic of local history, one village binding us together. He put before me his history of the Band and its predecessor about which I knew nothing until then and he was trusting enough to hand all his information over along with photographs and the souvenirs, these for copying and returning, and I promised that the copyright would remain his and I hoped to see it published in due course.

This commitment has been a long time being fulfilled but my wider historical interests in the village have taken my time. During those years I gathered in photographs of the Band at home and on its travels and now the two aspects can come together, some of the pictures having been used already in my local history books. I have also used the recollections of B. P. Sergeant, a local history enthusiast, but the foundation of this story is Arthur Scrivener's in its meticulous detail, long delayed but timed to coincide with one hundred years of dedicated activity of which he would have been proud and delighted.

Equally he would have welcomed the Brass Band Format summary by bandsman C. J. Palmer here included. Arthur's story continues to the Band's triumph of 1955. The photographic expertise of Vernon Place has been invaluable to this book.

Anthony Day
Wicken
May 2011

The beginnings of Wicken Band

From early times self-entertainment for country dwellers had its limitations. Any music had to come from homemade instruments very limited in scope. The human voice provided the better sounds for work and restricted play and if there was a rhythm to the work the singers picked it up. Even the sound of the tractor in my early days got their drivers singing, the most hearty giving vent to his religious beliefs in hymns that could be heard at some distance.

Coming in early were fiddlers, sometimes used in company with a serpent in the small musicians' gallery in churches and if there was a fiddler in the village the dancing was truly on, soon to be extended by tin whistles, concertinas and accordions. I had an uncle with a collection of these, all too neglected since his young days, but at my urging he brought forth an accordion to play a few stumbling tunes at Christmas, sending me away at last with the gift of a concertina that should have done more for my musical education.

The spirit of self-entertainment grew from the acquisition of these instruments and on Christmas Day in Wicken before the war young bachelors not held to their firesides toured the village with singing accompanied by band instruments, concertinas, accordions and mouth organs, all for the food and drink we cared to serve them. Mouth organists grew in number and many a child tried his luck with a sixpenny job from Woolworth's, only to see and hear the instrument played well during the brief existence of the Wicken Mouth Organ Band in the 1930s.

The construction of village halls gave a great boost to public entertainment from within and that at Wicken, built in 1887 as a second and more accessible church but soon in use for concerts and meetings, was made to last with modifications.

But long before that when the meeting places were the church and chapels, a group of men got together to form a brass band. 1836 was the year in which the first published music for brass bands appeared; indeed it was the year when the term 'brass band' first became acceptable as applying to a regular ensemble. The next hundred years became the golden era for brass bands, climaxing with the British championships at the ill-fated Crystal Palace.

Brass band music evolved through instrumental changes. Essential at first were the clarinet – which is still so with military bands – and the flute, reed instruments that were made of brass more often than not. Then the keyed bugle (Kent bugle) that played all the notes of the chromatic scale ousted the clarinet, but what was needed was a mechanism that could instantaneously add to or subtract from the length of tubing in order to change the pitch of the harmonic series and this mechanism was the valve, invented around 1814 and incorporated initially into the designs of horns and cornets.

The most significant change for the brass bands was the arrival of the clarinet which became as vital to them as the violin to classical orchestras. Developed from the post horn in about 1828, the cornet also displaced the French horn, but the trombone that originated in the fifteenth century also became integral to brass bands, its original valves giving way to the slide, two tenors and one brass being the norm today. The euphonium first appeared in about 1843.

But well before the spread of ensembles in so many of our towns and large villages the village of Wicken made its entry into the genre. Their centre was to be the Wesleyan Chapel, built in the 1820s, lasting until 1910 then replaced by a new. Sixteen men of the parish, mainly farm workers on poverty wages, vowed to acquire the necessary instruments to form their Wicken Wesleyan Brass Band, their formative meeting taking place in the chapel on 19 October 1869.

It was to hold its practice sessions in the chapel on Tuesday evenings and at the home of the elected bandmaster, Thomas Palmby, on an evening convenient to all. Mr Palmby lived at Afterways on the Stretham Road where he had a shed large enough for the purpose. Here follows the rules for members, some of them illiterate and needing to learn to read music, as set down by them, with no corrections to their spelling or punctuation:

'Rule one: All members on admission, pay three shillings entrance.

Rule two: All members meet to practice at the chapel on Tuesday Night at the appointed time of 7 o'clock if not there before 8 o'clock to pay 1d fine unless lawfully detained.

Rule 3: All members are to pay their weekly Subscriptions as shall be agreed to.

Rule 4: That no member of this band take any of the band instruments to play at the Public House (nor with any other person or Persons belonging to the other band, that is Wicken Band. If he do fined 6d. [Note that this appears in the original Rules but was crossed out]

Rule 5: Any who brake or damage his instrument to make it good as far as Possible, and any one who fail to comply with these Rules and get weary of the Band the Secretary shall call upon him and he shall give up his Musical Instrument to him.

Rule 6: All questions shall be settled by A Majority.

The names of the Members of the band Agreeing to the foregoing Rules – Signed this day October 19th 1869.

William Palmby

Walter Bishop

Thomas Palmby

Robert Scrivener   X

William Scrivener

John Bailey

William Cook   X

Charles Westrope

Robert Simpkin

James Layton

Hockley Bishop

David Taylor   November 1869

Isaac Taylor

James Bailey   January 4th 1870

Solomon Bailey   This day February 1st 1871

Joshua Bailey'

Octo 19 1869

The Rules of the Band Called the Wesleyan Methodist Amateur Brass Band

Rule 1st all members on admission pay 3 shillings entrance

Rule 2nd all Members meet to Practice at the Chapple on a Tuesday Nights at the appointed time 7 Oclock if not thair before 8 Oclock to Pay a fine unless lawfully Detained

Rule 3rd all Members are to pay thair weekly subscriptions as shall be agreed to

Rule 4 That no Member of this Band take any of the Band Instruments to play at the Public House nor ~~with any other Power or Persons belonging to~~ ~~other Band that is forbidden~~ ~~Band~~ if he do fine 6

Rule 5 any one who Brake or damage his Instrument to make it good as far as Possible, and any one who fail to comply with those Rules and get weary of the Band the secretary shall call upon him and he shall give up his Musical Instrument to him

Rule 6 All questions shall be settled bt Majority

The Names of the Members of the Band Agreeing to the foregoing Rules

Signed This Day Octo 19/1869
William Palmby Secretary
Walter Bishop
Thomas Palmby
Robt Scrivener
William Scrivener
John Bailey
William Cook
Charles Westrope
Robert Simpkin
James Taylor
Hockley Bishop
David Taylor Nov 9 1869
Isaac Taylor 1869
James Bailey Jany 4th 1870
Solomon Bailey This day Feby 14 1871
Joshua Bailey

The original formation document for the Wicken Wesleyan Brass Band

The Wicken Wesleyan Brass Band existed for more than twenty years, performing at the heart of the celebration in Wicken for Queen Victoria's Golden Jubilee in 1887. They led a parade from Cross Green consisting of the day school children and those from the church Sunday school and the Primitive and Wesleyan Sunday schools. The turnout reached above two hundred who followed the Band into North Street and back to enter Isaac Aspland's field, The Weights, then and later used for local sporting and leisure events. There followed at four pm tea for children and another for widows, widowers and aged couples in Mr Aspland's new cart sheds, this suitably prepared and decorated patriotically for the occasion. At five pm there was a public tea costing threepence per person in the vicarage garden and in the later evening sporting events continued followed by a firework display and the release of balloons, the day concluded by the Band playing the national anthem.

Thus the difference made by the presence of a band in its own parish, each community served by that or not at all for such an occasion. But, alas, it had ceased functioning long before the Diamond Jubilee of 1897, making it a more muted occasions, marked principally by the opening of the Diamond Jubilee Cottages built from local public contributions. Four years on, the coronation of Edward VII had no musical backing, the bands in neighbouring communities all held their own celebrations. But with the coming of the coronation of George V in June 1911 the absence of music for the occasion was felt acutely.

The need to counter this sent a buzz round the village that brought out a number of home bred musicians who vowed to lead a procession to church and back, come what may. We shall never know what sounds they made together but there were memories of the older band for comparison. The instruments brought forward were one cornet and one euphonium from the old band, two piccolos, one tin whistle, one flageolet, one bass drum and one kettledrum from the old band, one violin and the Wesleyan Chapel harmonium, this to be carried in a cart drawn by hefty lads with Jemima Houghton at the keys.

Rehearsals worthy of the name there were none but there was reported improvement on the way and once back in the field in Butts Lane (now Drury Lane) made ready for sporting events the musicians found greater unity rendering a few tunes. Indeed they aroused their own enthusiasm for more and better and when the word spread that they were to persevere together a collection was made on the field hopefully towards the cost of a new brass band for the village. Uplifted, the musicians soon agreed to call it the Wicken Coronation Band.

Enthusiasm remained high and a few days on a meeting was called and the Band was inaugurated under the title suggested. There were no fewer than 22 members of very limited experience along with their first patron, the Reverend Ernest Dibben, a bachelor whose stipend had to stretch to include three sisters living under his roof. However, he was not without means and once he was elected the Band's first president he offered to lend the money needed for the Band's first instruments, this free of interest.

It took but a short time to acquire the instruments from a firm in Euston Road, London, at a cost of £35. In two years through thrift and payment from engagements the vicar's money was returned. Impressed further by the dedication and the evident progress of the Band under its first bandmaster, Walter Bishop, the vicar offered to lend the money to acquire their first uniforms, with the same conditions. The players gladly accepted and the uniforms were duly purchased from the firm of

⚜ WICKEN ⚜
Coronation Sports

WILL BE HELD IN

Mr. W. O. Bullman's Grass Field,

BUTTS LANE,

JUNE 22nd, 1911.

Races for All
YOUNG AND OLD.

Treasurer - -	Mr. R. M. TREEN.
Chairman - -	„ P. J. WALLING.
Secretary - -	„ J. ANDREWS.

Committee:

Messrs. R. ASPLAND, J. BUTCHER, W. BARNES,
J. BULLMAN, R. MOTT, W. BARTON, A. BISHOP,
J. GRANFIELD, A. TAYLOR.

Judges:

Mr. G. TOWNSEND, J.P., C.C., and Mr. R. M. TREEN.

Starter:—Mr. J. ANDREWS.

This Programme is subject to Alteration.

Price One Half Penny.

RACES FOR CHILDREN.

AT 1.30 P.M.

1. Boys	....	under 5 years	....	3 Prizes.
2. Girls	....	under 5 „	....	3 „
3. Boys	....	over 5 to 7 years	....	3 „
4. Girls	....	over 5 to 7 „	....	3 „
5. Boys	....	over 7 to 9 „	....	3 „
6. Girls	....	over 7 to 9 „	....	3 „
7. Boys	....	over 9 to 11 „	....	3 „
8. Girls	....	over 9 to 11 „	....	3 „
9. Boys	....	over 11 to 13 years	....	3 „
10. Girls	....	over 11 to 13 „	...	3 „
11. Boys and Girls	over 13 to 14 „		....	6 „
12. Race for Boys	over 14 to 16 „		....	3 „
13. Race for Girls	over 14 to 16 „		....	3 „
14. Race for Cookery Girls who have left School.				
15. Reel Threading Competition for Boys over 16 years. 200 yds.				
16. Reel Threading Competition for Girls over 16 years, 150 yds.				

DURING THE DAY

Selections on the Gramophone.

Daylight Balloon Ascents

Kindly given by MR. MOTT.

⚜ **CHILDREN'S TEA AT 4.30 P.M.** ⚜

"God Save the King."

All Seniors entering for Races
should hand their entries in to
any of the Stewards on or
before June 20th.

⚜

The decision of the Judges to
be final.

SENIOR RACES.

		PRIZES.		
AT 5.30 P.M.		1st.	2nd.	3rd.
1. Nail-driving Competition for Ladies		3/-	2/-	1/-
2. Bicycle Race on Plank	....	3/-	2/-	1/-
3. The Ball and Bottle Competition	....	3/-	2/-	1/-
4. Veterans' Race, from 50 years upwards		3/-	2/-	1/-
5. Bran Pie Race	....	3/-	2/-	1/-
6. Ladies' Tortoise Bicycle Race, 50 yards		3/-	2/-	1/-
7. Gents' Needle Threading Race, 200 yards		3/-	2/-	1/-
8. Tug of War, married v. single, 11 each side		11/-	—	—
9. Ladies' Egg and Spoon Race, 50 yards		2/6	1/6	1/-
10. Gents' Tortoise Bicycle Race, 200 yards		3/-	2/-	1/-
11. Middle Age Race, from 35 years to 50		3/-	2/-	1/-
12. Mallet and Peg Competition	....	3/-	2/-	1/-
13. Gents' Sack Race	....	4/-	3/-	2/-
14. 100 Yards Flat Race	....	2/6	1/6	1/-
15. 220 „ „	....	3/-	2/-	1/-
16. 440 „ „	....	4/-	3/-	1/6
17. Obstacle Race „	....	5/-	3/-	2/-

18. **Decorated Bicycle Competition (Ladies').**

1st Prize, given by Mr. J. Bailey, of Esham. Gold Brooch, value 8/6.		
2nd Prize	... ...	Oil Lamp.
3rd Prize	... ...	Bicycle Pump.

19. **Decorated Bicycle Competition (Gents').**

1st Prize, given by Mr. Pollard, of Esham.		Gas Lamp.
2nd Prize	... ...	Cycle Cape.
3rd Prize	... ...	Bicycle Pump.

20. Good Night Race	...	....	5/- 3/- 2/-	

Programme for the day 1911

The Band's first march 1911

The Band's first march to church for Addenbrookes Hospital Fund 1911

The Band's first march to church for Addenbrookes Hospital Fund 1911

1912
Back, left to right: Arthur Bishop, Oswald Bailey, Harry Page, Bob Taylor, Walter Bishop (bandmaster), Arthur Scrivener, Joe Clay, Jim Andrews, William Scrivener.
Seated: Charlie Avey, Albert Taylor, Ernie Bailey, Nathan Norman, Billy Norman, David Bailey, George Barton, Bob Nixon.
Front: Cecil Bailey, Billy Avey, Clarence Bailey, George Avey, William Granfield.

10

Beevers of Huddersfeld at a cost of £32 and 10 shillings. Once again the loan was paid back in good time, indeed, within 18 months. So by 1913 the Wicken Coronation Band was outfitted and complete.

First uniforms 1913
Back, left to right: Billy Norman, Ernie Bailey, Cecil Bailey, Albert Scrivener, Bob Taylor, Walter Bishop (bandmaster), Jo Clay, William Scrivener, Jim Andrews, Oswald Bailey, George Barton.
Middle: Arthur Scrivener, Charlie Avey, Nathan Norman, Olley Bullman, Rev. E. Dibben, Bill Norman, Percy Walling, Jethro Granfield, Bob Nixon, David Bailey.
Front: George Avey, Billy Avey, Clarence Bailey, William Granfield.

These uniforms were sent by rail from Huddersfield to Soham and were fetched to Wicken on 12 April 1913. They were worn for the first time at a fete and sports meeting in Burwell on Whitsun Saturday 1913, this in aid of ex-servicemen.

First music played after the Band's formation in 1911

First music played after the Band's formation in 1911

Sports day 1921

Standing, left to right: Luke Rumberlow, Henry Clay, Giles Bailey, George Avey, Reg Bailey, Bert Canham, George Barton, Albert Avey, Alec Simpkin, Harry 'Rocker' Norman.

Seated: Charlie Avey, Arthur Scrivener, Billy Avey, Nathan Norman, Joe Clay and Albert Taylor.

Kneeling: Arthur Andrews, Ernie Avey, Horace Clay.

For the first two Christmas mornings of the Band's existence the bandsmen met at The Black Horse at the head of Lode Lane to take in houses all the way to Padney, playing by each one. Then they proceeded to Upware playing carols for Band funds. They walked back along Spinney Bank to arrive home for tea.

On the first two Boxing Days the bandsmen met at The Maid's Head at 10 in the morning then walked across the fen footpaths to Burwell where they toured the village playing carols and collecting funds. After taking refreshment at The King William at the top of the causeway they returned home for tea around 5 o'clock.

The bandsmen were not spared their own contributions in cash. They each had to pay a shilling to join the Band and meet a subscription of a penny a week. They were fined for non-attendance at rehearsals unless they had a valid excuse for the Inside Committee, this consisting of the bandmaster and four bandsmen.

Transport to their engagements became an early problem. There was no bus services at first but they hired a vehicle for their journey to Manea in 1924, this described as the first bus service in the district. It belonged to a Mr Gleave of Fordham. It had a high body and could carry 16 passengers. To enter the vehicle the passengers had to climb in at the back up two iron steps, but there was at least a cloth cover to keep out the rain – for a while.

The bus had to make two journeys to get all the bandsmen and loyal supporters to Manea, the first load setting off at 6.30 in the morning, arriving at Manea at 8.45. There had been two stops to refill with water and the driver lost his way for a while. And the bus had to cool down at Manea before Mr Gleave could return for the other passengers.

Meanwhile those left waiting at Manea made a tour of the village then regaled themselves at a public house, there being entertained by an old man playing and dancing to a tin whistle. They roused to this and encouraged him to play two tin whistles at once while still dancing. The contest at Manea was due to start at 2 o'clock but the second load of bandsmen had still not arrived with half an hour to go. At last they arrived, their journey having been more eventful than the first. The passengers had to push the bus at Fisk's Hill in Soham and the driver had to 'rest it' twice. When it arrived it was steaming like a locomotive.

The march the Band had to play was Cottonopolis. The people of Manea lined the route as the bandsmen made their way to the church to perform. A few raucous voices rose above the applause but it in no way deterred the troupe, nor did it affect them as they moved on to the park for the 'selection' contest, their piece coming from Verdi's La Traviata. The adjudicator was Mr Nuttall of Irwell Springs in Lancashire who pleased the Wicken players by placing them third in this their first competitive attempt. Our bandsmen stayed on to enjoy the sports on this celebration day, a penny-farthing bicycle race pleasing them most. Then they faced the long journeys home, the second contingent reaching home near midnight. They would all have to rise by six in the morning, but with tales to tell of this first competitive venture.

The very backbone of Wicken Coronation Band became the Avey family. The mother was a Wicken woman, the father soon becoming a basket maker who came to weave the first instrument cases for the Band, he a founder member with his two eldest sons Billy and George who became known as Fiddler. When the youngest son, Roland, joined the Band his father, Charlie, had retired from it but

1924

Taken at the rear of The Sycamores, High Street, where they practised by permission of Mrs M. E. Rix. The Band had just competed in the Manea and Soham Band Contests

Back, left to right: Bert Canham, Alex Simpkin, Horace Clay, Luke Rumbelow, George Avey, Giles Bailey, Arthur Scrivener, Reg Hitch, Jack Nixon.

Middle: Albert Avey, Joe Clay, George Barton, Harry Norman, Ernie Avey, Charlie Avey, Darkie Bailey.

Front: Frank Nixon, Solomon Bailey.

Berrycroft Methodist Church, Soham at a garden fete, June 1929

Back, left to right: Cyril Avey, Ernie Avey, Giles Bailey, Horace Clay, Reg Hitch, Wilfred Day, Frank Barber, Joshua Bailey.

Front: Frank Avey, George Barton, Albert Avey, Arthur Scrivener (bandmaster), Denis Porter, Bob Porter, Bert Canham, George Bailey.

he made up seven brothers dedicated to brass music, each a musician to the core. Roland topped their individual achievements as a trombone player. Ernie (Giant), George (Fiddler), Albert (Ghurkha) and Billy who escaped a nickname in a village that loved them, made up the Wicken Jazz Band in the early nineteen-thirties along with Hartley Hawes on the banjo and Dorothy Jenkinson on the piano and we have no way of telling that it was other than the best of New Orleans. Ernie played the saxophone, George the cornet, Albert the drums and Billy the violin. The two other brothers in Wicken Band were Frank, without nickname, whose three sons Brian, Charles, and Bernard followed him into the Band, and Cyril (Twig) who played the trombone.

Walter Bishop, with a family precedent was elected the first bandmaster of Wicken Coronation Band. The William Scrivener standing at the extreme right in the 1912 photograph was not he of the first Band although of that family. The second William, sadly, was killed in the First World War.

Jethro Granfield, a man of considerable enterprise and no little talent (he created the wooden plaque in the Swaffam Fen Chapel commemorating the fallen in the first world war) succeeded Walter Bishop as bandmaster and his successors were as follows: William Avey, George Avey, Arthur Scrivener for six years, son of William of the first Band, Ernie Avey, George Avey again and Roland Avey, leading to a very long stint by Ernie Avey into the nineteen-seventies, at which time he had to plead for release as a coverted bandmaster. Sadly Ernie died soon afterwards, a gentle, perceptive man born to loyalty.

Outside conductors of greater experience were engaged for various contests. Robert Austin, bandmaster of Cambridge Town Band, coached and conducted Wicken Band for the contest at Sennowe Park, Fakenham, in 1932 and F. J. Talbot of Soham Comrades Band was engaged to tutor and conduct all other contests in which Wicken Band participated from 1933 and post-war into the nineteen-fifties and, indeed, to the pinnacle of their achievement in 1955. On Easter Monday in 1958 at St Andrew's Church, Norwich, Mr Talbot became the first person to receive the award for playing standards in the regions. When Band practices were held in the yard of The Maid's Head at Wicken and Mr Talbot was at the helm the locals would gather to catch his pertinent and often amusing comments.

Although Billy Avey was a founder member of the Band and was playing with it into an advanced age, he left the village for a spell and clocked up fewer years of playing than Horace Clay whose service extended to 70 playing without a break. Giles Bailey, a brilliant cornet player always entrusted with the Last Post under the church tower on Armistice Sunday, was another long-server whose three daughters became the first female members of the ensemble in Wicken. Apart from Ernie Avey other long-servers include Wilfred Day and later Bill Jeffries while Colin Clay who, like his father, started playing with the Band at the age of 11, saw the century out as a player.

Outstanding among its presidents was Alec Simpkin, elected in 1926, who steered the Band through more than one crisis and who originally was a player, presiding into the nineteen-seventies. During the pre-war years the Band concerts in the Village Hall were essential entertainment, backed up by performers on stage, the Hall packed to the walls, kept warm enough by two iron stoves and illuminated by paraffin lamps.

Long before there was a National Health Service the standard way of raising funds for hospitals and nurses was through grand parades known as Hospital Sundays, these generally timed to coincide

Wicken Coronation Silver Prize Band, June 1939

Back, left to right: Ronald Clay, Reg Hitch, Cyril Avey, Clifford Nixon, Roland Avey, Percy Bird, Fred Bailey.

Middle: Giles Bailey, Horace Clay, Charlie Weight, Arthur Bailey, Bob Porter, Leslie Pamment.

Front: Frank Avey, Albert Avey, Wilfred Day, Ernie Avey (bandmaster), Billy Avey, George Avey, Bert Canham.

Wicken Band on the concert platform at Sennowe Park, Fakenham, Norfolk in June 1935, guest conductor, Robert Austin

with the town or village feasts and fairs, calendar dates as eagerly awaited as Christmas and hugely attended. Wicken's two-day celebration was May 13 and 14 with the church parade on the nearest Sunday.

But the big event hereabouts was at Soham in June bringing thousands to the streets and dressed up for the occasion, assured of being photographed from the vantage points from the eighteen-nineties until the Second World War which killed the events. Here is the typical turnout for 1932:

1. Soham Comrade Silver Prize Band
2. Soham British Legion
3. Fordham British Legion
4. Isleham and Mildenhall Bands
5. Soham and District Fire Brigades
6. Nurses Hospital Van
7. Oddfellows Club and Banner (Star of Charity Lodge)
8. Shepherds' Club (Providence Lodge L.A.D.S.)
9. Star of Providence
10. United Brethren
11. Wicken Coronation Band
12. Boys Brigade and Life Boys
13. Anchor Slate Club Decorated Car
14. Salvation Army Band
15. Soham Motor Ambulance

Hospital Sunday Parade 1933

Horace Turner Clay, the Band's longest serving player

The Band in June 1936 at Wicken Vicarage

Back row: left to right: George Rumbelow, Dick Bailey, Bill Barnes, Giles Bailey, Horace Clay, Arthur Bailey, Wilfred Day, Fred Bailey, Roland Avey, Joe Clay, Robert Canham, William Day.

Middle: Jimmy Clay, Cyril Avey, Clifford Nixon, Joshua Bailey, Reg Hitch, Percy Bird, Bob Porter, Ron Clay, Arthur Scrivener, Billy Avey, Sidney Barton.

Front: Bert Canham, Frank Avey, Martin Bailey, George Barton, Ernie Avey (bandmaster), Fred Talbot (coach), Alec Simpkin, Reverend Ernest Harrison, George Avey, Albert Avey.

This photograph was taken to celebrate the Band's cup win at Reepham in the Cawstom and District Brass Band Contest Section B, but it was also their silver jubilee.

On the day the Reepham Bandsmen's Challenge Cup was won by Soham Comrades Band. The first test for Wicken Band was the march Cottonopolis, winning them second prize (cash ten shillings!). In the selection contest (class C) their test piece was 'In days of old' gaining them second prize again (cash two pounds). For these they were conducted by maestro Fred Talbot.

Decorated Wagon 1930s

Post-war practice on The Weights, a field offered for sports

Transport where it can be found

Wicken Hospital Sunday Parade 1922

Hospital Sunday March 1930s

Crowd at Soham Hospital Sunday Parade 1929

Wicken Jazz Band, 1930
Left to right: Ernie Avey, George Avey, Albert Avey, Hartley Hawes, Billy Avey, Dorothy Jenkinson

Charlie Avey, basket maker

The seven Avey brothers of Wicken Band
Left to right: Billy, Rolly, Frank, Ernie (bandmaster), Albert, Cyril, George, 1951

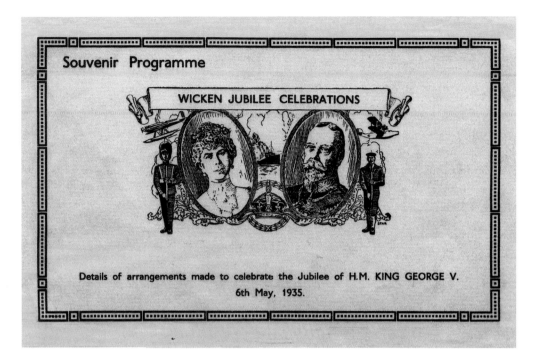

Souvenir Programme

WICKEN JUBILEE CELEBRATIONS

Details of arrangements made to celebrate the Jubilee of H.M. KING GEORGE V.
6th May, 1935.

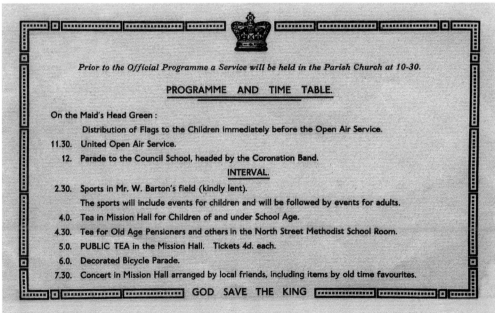

Prior to the Official Programme a Service will be held in the Parish Church at 10-30.

PROGRAMME AND TIME TABLE.

On the Maid's Head Green :

   Distribution of Flags to the Children immediately before the Open Air Service.

11.30.   United Open Air Service.

  12.   Parade to the Council School, headed by the Coronation Band.

INTERVAL.

2.30.   Sports in Mr. W. Barton's field (kindly lent).

   The sports will include events for children and will be followed by events for adults.

4.0.   Tea in Mission Hall for Children of and under School Age.

4.30.   Tea for Old Age Pensioners and others in the North Street Methodist School Room.

5.0.   PUBLIC TEA in the Mission Hall.   Tickets 4d. each.

6.0.   Decorated Bicycle Parade.

7.30.   Concert in Mission Hall arranged by local friends, including items by old time favourites.

GOD SAVE THE KING

Wicken Jubilee Celebration, 1935: programme

Celebration of the Coronation, 1937

Enthusiasm for competitive playing grew in Wicken Band. In 1923 they had gained third prize in a march contest at Soham, then came their eventful trip to Manea in 1924 bringing them another third prize. Taking breath to achieve more they became very active competitively in the nineteen-thirties. They were unplaced in their debut in the junior section as Crystal Palace in 1933. Then came second prize in Section C of the East Anglian Brass Band contest at Sennowe Park, Fakenham, Norfolk in 1933.

Before the 1936 contests the Wicken and New Buckenham Bands were graded to Section B due to the shortage of bands in that section. Then followed: second prize Section B in the East Anglian Brass Band Contest held at the Cambridge Guildhall, where the winners were Haverhall Co-operative Band.

It continues: First Prize and Cup Section B in the Sawston and District Brass Band Contest played under East Anglian rules – 1936. The Band also played in Section A on the same day but were unplaced, indicating the competition they might have to face in the future.

. PROGRAMME .

4-0 p.m.   Children's Tea in the Mission Hall.   (Free).

4-30 ,,   Tea for the older residents in the North Street Methodist School Room.   (Free).

5-15 ,,   Public Tea in the Mission Hall.   Tickets 4d.   (Please obtain your ticket early).

6-15 ,,   Carnival Procession and Fancy Dress Parade.

7-15 ,.   Concert in the Mission Hall arranged by the local Committee.

(Free).

There will be an interval for the reception of the King's Broadcast.

God Save the King.

. PROGRAMME .

9-10 a.m.   The Coronation Prize Band will assemble and parade to the Church.

9-30 ,,   Divine Service in the Parish Church.

10-30 ,,   Presentation of Flags to the children.
Councillor R. L. Fuller, J.P., will unveil the seat placed on the Green to commemorate the Coronation.

11-0 ,,   (a) Cricket Match arranged by the Sports Club.
(b) Mr. H. Barnes will arrange for the reception of the Abbey Service in the Mission Hall.

12-15 p.m.   Presentation of Beakers to children of and under school age in the Council School.

2-0 ,,   Sports for children and adults in Mr. Barton's field (kindly lent). The Coronation Prize Band will be in attendance.

On Good Friday 1937 Wicken gained Second Prize in the East Anglian Brass Band Contest Section B held at the Cambridge Guildhall where the winners were Dereham British Legion Band. At this time the Wicken players were being prepared by the worthy F. J. Talbot and the evidence is clearly there in their improvement in competitions as follows:

- First Prize and Cup: East Anglian Band Quartet Contest held at Thetford, Norfolk in 1936
- First Prize and Cup: East Anglian Brass Band Contest held at Thetford, Norfolk in 1937.

But from 1939 there were no band contests until 1947 when many bands were depleted. Wicken Band lost but one of its players in the war, this but eight days before the armistice. Indeed, his mother received news of the end of the war before that of her son's death. Arthur Scrivener paid tribute thus:

'Frederick William Bailey aged twenty-three years, the son of Mr and Mrs George Bailey of Afterways, Wicken, was killed in action on the 29th April 1945 in Germany, a fine young man over six feet tall attached to the Grenadier Guards and a fine cornet player in Wicken Coronation Silver Prize Band before he voluntarily joined the army.

When news of his death reached his parents on 12th May 1945 peace has been signed three days previous on 9th May.

Fred, as he was known to bandsmen and villagers alike, was liked and loved by all who knew him and the entire village mourned his loss. The Band lost a fine young player and the village one of its finest sons. Fred is buried in the Becklingen War Cemetery, Saltau, Germany.'

Grenadier Guardsman Fred Bailey (1922-45)

Wicken Band after 1945

Post-war Wicken Band was graded afresh to enter Section C, but they soon began to advance as the following list of awards shows:

- First Prize and Cup Section C East Anglian Band Contest held at Norwich in 1947
- Second Prize Hymn Tune Contest open to all bands held at Norwich in 1947
- First prize and Cup Section C Norfolk Band festival held at Reepham in 1947 and Second Prize and Cup Section B Norfolk Band Festival at the same event
- Second prize Section B East Anglian Band Contest at Norwich in 1948
- First Prize and Cup Section B Norfolk Band Festival held at Fakenham in 1948
- First Prize and Cup Section B East Anglian Band Contests held at Norwich on Easter Monday in 1949
- First Prize and Cup Section B Norfolk Band Festival held at Reepham in 1949
- Third Prize Section A Littleport Band Contest held at Highfield, Littleport in 1951
- First Prize and Cup Section A Littleport Band Contest held at Highfield, Littleport in 1952
- First Prize and Cup Section A East Anglian Band Contest held at Norwich in 1953
- Third Prize Championship Section, East Anglian Brass Band Contest held at Norwich in 1954
- First prize and Cup and the Championship of East Anglia held at Norwich in 1955
- Individual Prize at the Norfolk Band Festival in 1948 in Fakeham. Roland Avey, youngest of the seven Avey brothers playing for Wicken Band, was awarded the Gold Medal for being the best trombone player.

Wicken Band at this time was made up of Wicken players, an entirely local enterprise from a population of around seven hundred. Their ascent to the Championship of East Anglia was an astounding achievement, a true tale of dedication and ambition. If there were one or two abstentions in 1955 their opponents all came from much bigger communities. Pride and ambition showed early and the players had agreed in 1933 to sacrifice some £200 from their own pockets for a new set of silver plated instruments, the money to be restored to them through engagements and collections and it was this that gave rise to their extended title of Wicken Coronation Silver Prize Band.

Those proudly-worn first uniforms were losing their lustre after nearly twenty years, so they were replaced in 1932, the new matching the pattern of the Dragoon Guards with white stripes across the chest, gradually narrowing to waist level, with matching hat and trousers. After a similar period the change was to another Guards pattern, the tunic scarlet with matching hat and trousers.

This was the proud aspect, but hidden behind the rousing and light-hearted entertainment they provided was the sacrifice of time for labouring men who in these formative days of the Band earned but 12 shillings a week in winter and 13 shillings in summer. Coming up to the Second World War the weekly wage for landworkers was but 30 shillings with double wages only for the long, exhausting hours of harvest with piecework wages for nurturing and harvesting the sugar beet. Hardly without exception men grew much of their food as possible on their gardens and allotments, meaning their time was at a premium. If the joy of making music was their reward there were prolonged periods of practice to fill their limited time.

While, since the war, bands in neighbouring, and much larger, villages have folded, Wicken's has persevered, surviving through crises of opinion and fluctuating members and dependence on players from the outside. The native population has continued to diminish and, of course, there is so much to keep people entertained at home and ready transport to take them away.

Support from an unshakable band of supporters has been vital as have the long list of vice-presidents together with legacies and gestures such as that in 1976 by Martin Webster and Robert Tyler who offered two challenge cups to be used as the Band wished.

When, after such long service as the bandmaster, Ernie Avey resigned it opened the way for non-local Alan Shaw to take over, this at a time of disharmony in the ranks to be followed by quick changes. Barry Peacock became the bandmaster with Brian Avey, son of Frank, as his deputy. By 1987 their successor was P. Green who soon gave way to Wicken's Derek Bullman in whose first year the vice-presidents contributed a cup to be offered for the new under-tens classes at Witchford.

THE EAST ANGLIAN BRASS BAND ASSOCIATION

Long Service Certificate

awarded to

GILES BAILEY

IN RECOGNITION OF LONG AND DEVOTED SERVICE

TO THE BRASS BAND MOVEMENT

Alicia Austin .Vice.President . Geoffrey ala .Vice.Chairman

Olive Pratt . Secretary   19 . 4   1965.

Long Service Certificate: Giles Bailey

145

PARISH OF WICKEN.

▼

VICTORY DAY CELEBRATIONS.

TO BE HELD

On Saturday June 8th, 1946.

Hobbs, King & Parr, Soham

Victory Day
Celebrations, 1946,
Programme

PROGRAMME
OF
EVENTS.

2-15 p.m.	Service at the War Memorial. Children to proceed to the Sports Field.
3-0 p.m.	Childrens' Sports on Mr. Barton's Field.
5-15 p.m.	Childrens' Tea at Wicken School.
6-15 p.m.	Childrens' Fancy Dress Parade.
7-30 p.m.	Victory Dance in Wicken School. In aid of School and Youth Club Funds.

The music for the Service at the Memorial and before the Sports will be provided by

WICKEN BAND.

Childrens' Sports.

PROGRAMME
—

1	100 yds. (Handicap) Flat Race for Boys 11 to 14.
2	100 yds. (Handicap) Flat Race for Girls 11 to 14.
3	50 yds. Egg and Spoon Race. Under 11.
4	50 yds. Flat Race. 5 to 7.
5	80 yds. Three-legged Race for Girls 11 to 14.
6	80 yds. (Handicap) Flat Race for Boys 7 to 11.
7	80 yds. (Handicap) Flat Race for Girls 7 to 11.
8	80 yds. Three-legged Race for Boys 11 to 14.
9	25 yds. Flat Race. Under 5.
10	50 yds. Sack Race. 11 to 14.
11	100 yds. Wheeling Bicycle Backwards. Open.
12	Potato Race. Open.
13	25 yds. Slow Bicycle Race. Open.
14	50 yds. Flag Race. Under 11.
15	100 yds. Skipping Race for Boys 11 to 14.
16	100 yds, Skipping Race for Girls 11 to 14.
17	80 yds. Skipping Race for Boys 7 to 11.
18	80 yds. Skipping Race for Girls 7 to 11.
19	25 yds. Wheelbarrow Race for Boys.
20	50 yds. Flag Race. 11 to 14.

Billy Avey (first baritone)

Wilfred Day (double bass)

Bill Jeffries (first bass)

John Bailey (solo cornet)

Developing a Youth Band

There was an increasing need of youngsters to join the Band and with Derek and Gary Bullman at the helm the seeds were sown for a separate Youth Band for which Gary was to be bandmaster. It came into being in 1989 bringing together 26 youngsters aged between nine and 19. They held practice nights separately with tuition from many members of the senior Band. There was also a beginners' class taking in five-year-olds and upwards in small groups of three or four, but for some of the children had already begun to play brass instruments in their schools and colleges, their further need being to prepare themselves to face an audience. These youngsters were soon being prepared to enter contests as soloists, in quartets or the whole Band and their success was swift and quite remarkable.

Under the conductorship of Derek Bullman, the Wicken Youth Band took first place in the Youth Section at the East Anglian Brass Band Association Contest in 1993 and 1995 and under the conductorship of Heather Finlayson (now Ickeringill) they became the Youth Band Champions of East Anglia in 1996. Later Sylvia Greenway became Youth Bandmaster and held the post until the Youth Band disbanded in 2008.

It was a remarkable period but youth numbers can never be guaranteed. Schooling takes the youngsters away and there were too few replacements to maintain it. Nevertheless a few from the Youth Band return when they can to swell the seniors.

Chris Taylor, a solicitor, having played with the Band for a few years, became a popular President at this time with Robin James his deputy and when Robin succeeded Tony Day became his deputy. By this time the Band had come under the baton of Ray Boulter, an experienced leader from Soham Town Comrades Band. In 1996 the senior Band attended a special event in Germany to celebrate the twinning of East Cambridgeshire with Kempen and a friendship link with Manheim. Later the favour was returned when the Manheim Band played in the village college at Soham.

Both Wicken Bands were flourishing to an almost unbelievable degree into the 21st century and the Youth Band came back from their performances at the Cromer and Sheringham Brass Contest in 1995, leaving their founder and conductor, Derek Bullman wondering if they left any trophies behind at all! The Band won five first prizes, five second prizes and three thirds. Jamie Clay, son of Colin, grandson of Horace the longest server, was outstanding at this time. The three generations played together for a time.

But glory time for the youngsters could not last. Keeping a settled group of young players together proved impossible. Soon a bigger problem came to be the need to refurbish the Band and it became a priority to apply for lottery money. Fund raising began hopefully to raise the necessary percentage to go with the application. Old band instruments, some used for between 30 and 40 years, had to be replaced and if the aimed-for sum had to be reduced the award was still substantial. The new instruments acquired were brass, necessitating a change to Wicken Coronation Brass Band. This injection of new hope was a just reward for a Band with a repertoire of more than 750 pieces of music on file ranging from championship choices through to modern numbers such as The Lion King from Walt Disney and pop music for the Beatles on.

A mix of senior and junior players with the trophy won at Ely in 1982, one still held by the Band until there is a chance to defend it

Back, left to right: Mrs Alan Watson, Alan Watson, Jim Baddock, Garry Watson, Valerie Bullman, Bill Jeffries, Colin Clay, Timothy Bullman.

Front: Adrian Ickeringill, Paul Richmond, Chris Finlayson, Derek Bullman, Duncan Smith, Jamie Clay, Heather Finlayson.

[Photo Len Edwards]

Into the 21st century

Ray Boulter left the Band leaving Derek Bullman to become conductor of both Bands, but soon he resigned to allow Ray Boulter to return. Meanwhile the senior Band had continued to compete with success in annual competitions, although they declined to enter the East Anglian Band Contest in 2001. Some dispute occurred between the bandmasters in 2002 leading to Derek Bullman's departure. His quartet from the Youth Band meanwhile, being Matthew Ralph, Gayle Bullman, Amy Houghton and Alice Logsby won first prize at the Cromer and Sheringham Solo Duets competition.

Problems persisted with having the two Bands. With youth members declining a decision sometime had to be reached as to which ensemble should have priority since several players aspired to playing for both. Enthusiasm was high among the youngsters for playing with the senior Band, a natural ambition when growing up.

In 2003 the new Band President, Laurence Finlayson, admitted the difficulty of getting a Band together, some players missing engagements. The government proposal to make all live performances licensable could prove detrimental to the Band and he urged all players to sign a petition sent by the British Federation of Brass Bands. He also said they were short on numbers for another trip to Germany. This at a time when former bandmaster Derek Bullman had received a certificate for the East Anglian Band Association for this work with brass bands. But in 2004 the trip the Germany was a success. And this was this year when Bill Jeffries and John Bailey received their awards for 50 years playing service from the East Anglian Band Association.

Still in 2004 Ray Boulter lamented the poor attendance at Band practice and he put the case that this must improve during the next six moths. Sadly however, Ray became ill and had to resign his position, Sylvia Greenway took over for five engagements only. It was put forward that the Youth Band practices should be moved to Wednesday evening to precede the senior practices, a further coming together after the youths had previously rented the Wesleyan Chapel. Robert Peacock, Band chairman and long a tower of strength to the Band, urged an approach to Isleham school, hopefully to enrol youngsters from there to swell the Youth Band.

All this indicated a rapid decline in youth players. In 2005 hope still remained in spite of members rising up into the senior band prematurely, if of necessity, to the seniors. But the youths competed at Sheringham winning second in junior duets, first in junior quintet and third in intermediate quartets. But 2007 became the most difficult the Bands had endured. A new bandmaster, Colin Thomas, was engaged but left early to work in China but with a promise to return after six months. Sadly, after temporary leadership, he never returned.

It was time of real struggle with poor attendances at their engagements and low turnout on practice nights that had already been reduced to fortnightly. With so few native players there was poor support for the Band's annual Christmas concerts but at the same time any concert put on by them at

Fordham's Victoria Hall filled it to capacity, their repertoire a revelation. Robert Peacock worked wonders to get in extra players for this concert, conducted by Lisa Jardine. A little earlier Tony Bligh conducted the Band but was short of experience for the job and the Youth Band was still going while Robert Peacock was working so strenuously to ensure the Band's survival.

Sylvia Greenway had taken on the role of bandmaster to the Youth Band some eight years before it folded in 2008. While it lasted it was a great achievement to maintain two bands within such a small village. With their latest bandmaster Wicken Coronation Brass Band have strengthened with news of former players coming back and enthusiastic new arrivals. High optimism reigned at the 2010 annual general meeting when Robert Peacock urged a return to the area competitions with Tim Hammond at the helm and the centenary in view.

It will also be the centenary of the second Wesleyan Chapel, the first having supplied the village with its own music so long ago.

Wicken Youth Band in the 1990s
Back row, left to right: Heather Finlayson, Jim Badcock (chairman), Derek Bullman (bandmaster), Pat Finlayson (secretary), Sylvia Greenway (teacher).
Second row: Sarah Burgess, Lucy O'Reilly, Jamie Clay, Paul Martin, Stephen GIlbey, Gareth Neal, Rachel Petersen.
Third row: Tim Bullman, teacher, Michael O'Reilly, Robert O'Reilly, Karen Lofts, Melissa Myhill, Claire Buck, Sean Thronhill, Gareth Buck.
Fourth row: Graham Mayes, Sarah Beckett, Laura Leonard, Kayleigh Beaton, Phillipa Sabberton, Emma Stratton, Simon Thompson.
Front: Emma Crick, Jamie Leonard, Gail Bullman. Jamie Gilbey, Shaun Myhill, Josh Schumann.
[Photo Vernon Place]

The Fiftieth Anniversary 1961

Back, left to right: Giles Bailey, Derek Bullman, John Bailey, Cyril Bullman, Arthur Bailey, John Eaglen, Leslie Pamment.

Middle: Ernie Avey, Bernard Avey, Joe Tennyson, Horace Clay, Richard Harding, Charlie Avey, Bill Handley, Vic Williams.

Front: Wilfred Day, Colin Cropley, Bill Leach, George Avey, Brian Avey, Frank Avey, Bill Jeffries.

The Seventy-Fifth Anniversary 1986

Back row, left to right: John Bailey, David Wright, Alan Watson, Gary Watson, John James, Charlie Wright.

Second row: Tim Bullman, Valerie Bullman, Laurie Green, Heather Finlayson, Rachel James, Garry Bullman, Colin Clay.

Front: Christopher Finlayson, Derek Bullman, Gillian Hollingshead, Barry Peacock, Phillip Green (bandmaster), Vic Williams, Bill Jeffries, Horace Clay, Jamie Clay. [Photo: Vernon Place]

Horace, Colin and Jamie are father, son and grandson. Horace's father was an early member of the Band.

This photograph by Vernon Place, himself a former member of the Band, was taken at a garden party in aid of the Wesleyan Chapel fund, preceding the Band's own fete on 30 August. It was also the new chapel's 75th anniversary, thus its centenary in 2011.

1993

Back, left to right: Ian Gilbey, Derek Bullman, Colin Clay, Chris Taylor, Jonathan Earl, Bill Jeffries, Jim Badcock, Gary Watson, Stuart Smith.

Second row: Michael O'Reilly, Gareth Neal, Stephen Bilbey, Robin Pearson, Rachel James, Timothy Bullman, Heather Finlayson.

Front: Anna Carter, David Fisher, Charlie Avey, Roy Boulter (bandmaster), Lucy O'Reilly, John Bailey, Paul Anderson, Valerie Watts, Secretary.

Taken in Ely.

The Band photographed in 1956, following their greatest achievement in 1955: Champions of East Anglia

Back row, left to right: Vic Williams, Charlie Wright, Arthur Bailey, John Bailey, Ernie Avey, Giles Bailey, Vernon Place, Brenda Bailey, Mary Bailey.

Second row: Derek Bullman, Billy Avey, Bernard Avey, Bob Porter, Horace Clay, Brian Diver, Leslie Pamment, Rolly Avey, Alan Nixon, Cyril Avey.

Front: Albert Avey, Wilfred Day, Frank Avey, Fred Talbot (bandmaster for the competition), George Avey, Brian Avey.

Wicken Coronation Band 2011

Back row, left to right: Ron Adkins, Benjamin Edwards, Sylvia Greenaway, Chloe French, Jamie Gilbey, Cedric Palmer, Steve Allsop.

Middle row: Lisa Burgess, Heather Ickeringill, Sam Palmer, Katie Ashton, Daniel Tuck, Sandra Rampley, Steve Moore, Robert Peacock, David Cameron.

Front row: Ted Tyler, Jock Muir, Tracey Needham, Laurence Finlayson (President), Graham Smith, Musical Director, Niki Williamson, Matt Rolfe, Carl Rolfe, Bill Jeffrey.

[Photo Vernon Place]

The Brass Band Format

The 'Standard Brass Band Instrumentation and Format

Prepared by C. J. Palmer

Whilst any number of instrumentalists may play in a brass band in all positions, the Standard Brass Band Instrumentation and Format is that as regulated and recognised by the National and Regional Brass Band Associations for contests and consists of a maximum of 25 instrumentalists plus percussion, made up as follows:

A complete breakdown of the instrumentation and parts they play is as follows.

Cornet section
One Eb soprano cornet
Four Bb solo cornets
One Bb repiano cornet
Two Bb 2nd cornets
Two Bb 3rd cornets

Horn section
One Bb flugel horn
One Eb 1st tenor horn
One Eb 2nd tenor horn

Baritones
One Bb 1st baritone
One Bb 2nd baritone

Euphoniums
One Bb solo euphonium
One Bb asst euphonium

Trombones
One Bb solo (or 1st) trombone
One Bb 2nd trombone
One G (or bass) trombone

Basses
One (or two) Bb basses plus
One BBb bass
Two Eb basses

Percussion
One/two

Cornet section
Eb soprano cornet:
One soprano player. Pitched in the key of 'G', a fourth higher than the other cornets and Bb instruments, it is sometimes referred to as 'the icing on the cake'. Can be very 'showy' in the hands of an accomplished player, adding embellishments and descants to the music. Has many incidental solo parts. Shares in harmonies and links with the solo cornets, solo tenor horn and sometimes with the euphonium, Eb basses and 'G' trombone.

Bb solo cornet:
Four solo cornet players. Equivalent to the violins in an orchestra, they consist of the principal cornet who leads the cornet section and who plays the incidental solo parts, the assistant principal who supports the principal and two tutti cornet players. The solo cornets take the lead melody and can have a very demanding workload which requires much stamina, hence four players.

Bb repiano cornet:
One repiano player. Shares in rhythms and harmonies with the 2nd and 3rd cornets and flugel horn as well as providing supporting link with the solo cornets which it often accompanies.

Two Bb 2nd and 3rd cornets:

Two 2nd cornet players and two 3rd cornet players. Arranged in harmony, these provide the rhythms together with the 1st and 2nd tenor horns, linking with the 2nd baritone and 2nd trombone. Shares contrapuntal rhythms with the bass section. Takes the lower part when in harmony with the solo cornets.

Horn section
Bb flugel horn:

One flugel horn player. Equivalent to the viola in an orchestra, it is larger than the cornet with a softer, mellower sound. Plays solo passages while also sharing its score and harmonising with the solo tenor horn, joining the repiano cornet in unison as well as accompanying the solo cornets.

Eb solo tenor horn:

One solo tenor horn player. Equivalent to the French horn in an orchestra and pitched in Eb, the solo horn shares in harmonies and in unison with the flugel horn, euphonium, 1st baritone, soprano cornets as well as joining the 1st and 2nd horns in rhythm work. Has incidental passages.

Eb 1st and 2nd tenor horn:

One 1st tenor horn player and one 2nd tenor horn player. Provides rhythms and harmonies with the 2nd and 3rd cornets also 2nd baritone and sometimes the 1st baritone and 2nd trombone. 1st tenor horn will sometimes support the solo horn while at other times three horns may play in harmony.

Euphonium and baritone section
Bb euphonium:

Two euphonium players. The euphonium is a unique instrument in that it is the only non-transposing instrument in the band which allows it to play in both the higher register (treble) and lower register (bass) by utilising its fourth value. The solo euphonium player, by definition, plays the incidental solo passages and is supported by the second euphonium player although they both play the same music. The euphonium supplies the link with the bass section and also shares the lead (melody) with the solo cornets while sometimes harmonising with the solo horn, solo trombone and soprano cornet. Will also accompany the basses and trombones, especially in marches.

1st Bb baritone:

One 1st baritone player. Slightly smaller than the euphonium, the baritone has a deeper sound than the tenor horn but not the richer, rounded deepness of the euphonium. However, the 1st baritone does a lot of work, sharing its part in places with the solo cornet, euphonium, trombone and bass sections. It may also find itself in harmony with the 2nd baritone and tenor horns in rhythmic passages and occasionally in solo passages.

2nd Bb baritone:

One 2nd baritone player. With the tenor horns, 2nd and 3rd cornets and 2nd trombone provides rhythms and harmonies while sometimes sharing its part with the 1st baritone. Now and again it may find itself playing a solo passage.

Trombone section

Solo (or 1st) Bb trombone:

One solo trombone player. Leads the trombone section, plays the incidental solos. Will share score with euphoniums and 1st baritone sometimes with solo cornets. With the trombone section shares the bass part, especially in marches.

2nd Bb trombone:

One 2nd trombone player. Accompanies the solo trombone and shares rhythm and harmony with 2nd and 3rd cornets, tenor horns and 2nd baritone. Sometimes accompanies basses, especially in marches.

Bass (or 'G') trombone:

One 'G' trombone player. The only instrument in the band whose part is written in the bass clef as opposed to all the others which are written in the treble clef. A much deeper sounds and range in the bass register than the Bb trombone; particularly effective in hymn tunes and marches (Almost growls!) Accompanies basses and Bb trombones but can be an independent instrument. Compliments the soprano cornet in the bass register.

Bass section

Bb bass*:

Two Bb bass players. By definition, plays the bass line and defines the rhythm with the 2nd and 3rd cornets, tenor horns, 2nd baritone and 2nd trombone. In harmony with the Eb bass and also with the 1st baritone, euphonium and trombones.

Eb bass:

Two Eb bass players. Again by definition, plays bass line. Pitched a fourth higher than the Bb bass enables it to play with and complete the link between the bass section and the euphonium. Supplies rhythms and harmonises with the Bb basses, euphonium, baritone and trombones. Compatible in duets/trios with Eb tenor horn, soprano cornet and 'G' trombone.

BBb bass*:

One BBb (double) bass player. The double Bb bass plays in a much lower register than the Bb bass giving it a depth of sound comparable to the 'G' trombone but not quite so harsh. Plays in harmony and unison with the Bb and Eb basses and 'G' trombone.

*Where a BBb bass player is used then only one Bb bass player is allowed unless of course there is only one Eb bass player, four bass players being the maximum.

Percussion:

One or two percussionists (dependant on what is required). Percussion today consists of a full drum kit, tampanis, tubular bells, glockenspiel … in fact almost anything including sandpaper!